MW01533821

The journal and planner for the
people who don't journal and plan.

DEDICATION & MESSAGE

To my kids and husband, for adding love, color and laughter to my life. To me, for turning struggles into growth and for being a d*mn good ugly crier.

And to you, dearest gentle reader, for picking up this journal & planner. May it inspire and guide you through your own journey of self-discovery and strength.

Table of Contents

3 Reasons Why You'll Love the 3-Minute Daily Mindset Journal and Planner

1. SIMPLEST THING YOU CAN DO TO BE HAPPIER AND MORE CONFIDENT.

It starts with a thought. According to the National Science Foundation, the average person has about 12,000 to 60,000 thoughts per day. Each of those thoughts lead to an emotion, and each emotion leads to an action. Sounds pretty simple, right?

Then the thoughts start racing. "Well, this just means I have more ideas and I take more productive action!" Not exactly, about 70% of those thoughts are usually negative. When these thoughts start to race, it creates a loop in the mind, preventing and invading your sense of peace and being extremely destabilizing where the driving emotion to an action becomes worry, fear, sadness, or anxiety, taking up a great deal of time and becoming self-consuming. So, not only are you not getting things done, but they are done poorly when they are. This can mean you're not acing that test because you got distracted and study time was cut short; you avoid the gym because you think what's the point? Or you sit there overthinking all the ways starting your own business is a "bad" idea, so you quit before getting started. This mind loop negatively impacts the efficiency and effectiveness of your actions as well as your confidence.

3 Reasons Why You'll Love the 3-Minute Daily Mindset Journal and Planner

This cycle chips away at your confidence. Because confidence comes from completing tasks successfully—consistently. We want choices to be made with good judgement that bring happiness, strength, peace, love and abundance.

Most people experience racing thoughts. Racing thoughts can come and go rarely, occur frequently or persist indefinitely. This race in the mind, especially negative ones, is the number one struggle for most people that causes stagnation and/or regression in their overall growth mentally, physically, and spiritually.

2. SCIENCE-BACKED WITH PROVEN PSYCHOLOGICAL PRINCIPLES.

Psychologists say the secret is 3-minutes. If there's something you're dreading or avoiding, try doing it for just three minutes. The first 3-minutes will snap you out of an avoidance mindset. And it's not just chores; the 3-minute rule works for fitness regimes, phobias and even social anxiety. Trials show that 3-minutes is the sweet spot—98% of participants pushed through and continued. The same also applies to starting each task on your to-do list for 3-minutes. Chances are you will complete it.

3 Reasons Why You'll Love the 3-Minute Daily Mindset Journal and Planner

The power of pen-to-paper. Writing by hand helps your brain. It's backed by science. A simple study conducted in 2015 with women aged 19-54 concluded that those that had written by hand versus typing on a keyboard or using an iPad to write words, were significantly better at recalling the words they had written. Handwriting engages multiple senses like touch, leading to deeper learning, sharper ideas, better decisions—and ultimately, better outcomes.

Science says gratitude attracts happiness. According to Harvard Health, gratitude is a powerful emotion that attracts positivity and greater happiness. Positivity is a mindset practice that affects every part of our being and that's why the journal section starts every morning with a positive affirmation and what you're grateful for. The reflection in the evening serves as a reminder and accountability check for your emotions, concluding your night with good things that occurred that day.

3. EASY WAY TO STAY CONSISTENT AND PRODUCTIVE.

Planner keeps you present. This planner section focuses only on what matters most—the tasks responsible for 80%

3 Reasons Why You'll Love the 3-Minute Daily Mindset Journal and Planner

of your day's progress. Staying present has been linked to more focus, greater self-esteem and self-awareness. As you train your mind to do these gratitude check-ins and tasks each day automatically, you will garner more and more confidence and momentum. Your life will improve.

This journal and planner has taken years for me to develop and has helped me tremendously. I hope it helps you too.

Thank you for your support.

-Gigi

DATE:

MORNING AFFIRMATION:

Keep these in the present. It should be as if it's already happening.

SEE AFFIRMATION GUIDE AT THE END OF BOOK for ideas.

I'M GRATEFUL FOR:

Be very specific. Write the simplest of pleasures. Examples:

"I'mgrateful for date night with my husband tonight. I'm grateful for my new coffee machine.

I'm grateful my daughter had a great first day of school yesterday."

DAILY GOALS

MANDATORY
(Everyday Stuff)

JOURNAL

WORKOUT

QUALITY TIME FAMILY/FRIEND

The small, non-negotiable habits

that keep you grounded.

Examples: workout, journal,

take vitamins, drink water.

DO NOW
(80% of Productivity)

These are the tasks that truly

matter today. They're tied to

your income, your purpose, your

peace—or your people. Break

up tasks in steps.

HOW TO
GUIDE
for the journal & planner

DO LATER
(But Still Important)

Not urgent—but needs your

attention soon. Writing them

keeps them off your mind—but

in your view.

Examples:

Plan Summer Trip

Start Podcast

Examples:

"MAIN TOPIC - Next Step"

JOB SEARCH - Edit Resume

BILLS - Pay Gas Bill

CLIENTS - Program Workouts

KIDS - Make Dentist Appt

EVENING REFLECTION: Good Things That Happened Today

Be very specific. Write the simplest of pleasures. Examples: " I had fun watching the

movie with my family today - we laughed so much!"

DATE:

MORNING AFFIRMATION:

_____

_____

I'M GRATEFUL FOR:

_____

_____

DAILY GOALS

MANDATORY

_____
JOURNAL
_____
WORKOUT
_____
QUALITY TIME FAMILY/FRIEND
_____
_____
_____
_____

DO LATER

_____
_____
_____
_____
_____
_____

DO NOW
(80% of productivity)

_____
_____
_____
_____
_____
_____
_____
_____
_____
_____
_____
_____
_____
_____
_____

EVENING REFLECTION: Good Things That Happened Today

_____

_____

DATE:

MORNING AFFIRMATION:

_____

_____

I'M GRATEFUL FOR:

_____

_____

DAILY GOALS

MANDATORY

DO NOW
(80% of productivity)

_____
JOURNAL
_____
WORKOUT
_____
QUALITY TIME FAMILY/FRIEND
_____

_____

_____

_____

DO LATER

_____

_____

_____

_____

_____

_____

EVENING REFLECTION: Good Things That Happened Today

_____

_____

DATE:

MORNING AFFIRMATION:

_____

_____

I'M GRATEFUL FOR:

_____

_____

_____

DAILY GOALS

MANDATORY

_____
JOURNAL
_____
WORKOUT
_____
QUALITY TIME FAMILY/FRIEND
_____

_____

_____

_____

DO LATER

_____

_____

_____

_____

_____

_____

DO NOW
(80% of productivity)

_____

_____

_____

_____

_____

_____

_____

_____

_____

_____

_____

_____

_____

EVENING REFLECTION: Good Things That Happened Today

_____

_____

DATE:

MORNING AFFIRMATION:

_____

_____

I'M GRATEFUL FOR:

_____

_____

DAILY GOALS

MANDATORY

_____
JOURNAL
_____
WORKOUT
_____
QUALITY TIME FAMILY/FRIEND
_____
_____
_____
_____

DO LATER

_____
_____
_____
_____
_____
_____
_____

DO NOW
(80% of productivity)

_____
_____
_____
_____
_____
_____
_____
_____
_____
_____
_____
_____
_____

EVENING REFLECTION: Good Things That Happened Today

_____

_____

DATE:

MORNING AFFIRMATION:

_____

_____

I'M GRATEFUL FOR:

_____

_____

_____

DAILY GOALS

MANDATORY

_____
JOURNAL
_____
WORKOUT
_____
QUALITY TIME FAMILY/FRIEND
_____

_____

_____

_____

DO LATER

_____

_____

_____

_____

_____

DO NOW
(80% of productivity)

_____

_____

_____

_____

_____

_____

_____

_____

_____

_____

_____

_____

EVENING REFLECTION: Good Things That Happened Today

_____

_____

DATE:

MORNING AFFIRMATION:

_____

_____

I'M GRATEFUL FOR:

_____

_____

DAILY GOALS

MANDATORY

_____

_____ JOURNAL _____

_____ WORKOUT _____

QUALITY TIME FAMILY/FRIEND

_____

_____

_____

_____

DO LATER

_____

_____

_____

_____

_____

_____

DO NOW
(80% of productivity)

_____

_____

_____

_____

_____

_____

_____

_____

_____

_____

EVENING REFLECTION: Good Things That Happened Today

_____

_____

MORNING AFFIRMATION:

_____

_____

I'M GRATEFUL FOR:

_____

_____

DAILY GOALS

MANDATORY

_____
JOURNAL
_____
WORKOUT
_____
QUALITY TIME FAMILY/FRIEND
_____
_____
_____
_____
_____

DO LATER

_____
_____
_____
_____
_____
_____

DO NOW
(80% of productivity)

_____
_____
_____
_____
_____
_____
_____
_____
_____
_____
_____
_____
_____

EVENING REFLECTION: Good Things That Happened Today

_____

_____

DATE:

MORNING AFFIRMATION:

_____

_____

I'M GRATEFUL FOR:

_____

_____

_____

DAILY GOALS

MANDATORY

_____
JOURNAL
_____
WORKOUT
_____
QUALITY TIME FAMILY/FRIEND
_____

_____

_____

_____

DO NOW
(80% of productivity)

_____

_____

_____

_____

_____

_____

_____

DO LATER

_____

_____

_____

_____

_____

_____

_____

_____

_____

_____

EVENING REFLECTION: Good Things That Happened Today

_____

_____

DATE:

MORNING AFFIRMATION:

_____

_____

I'M GRATEFUL FOR:

_____

_____

_____

DAILY GOALS

MANDATORY	DO NOW
	(80% of productivity)

MANDATORY

_____

JOURNAL
_____
WORKOUT
_____
QUALITY TIME FAMILY/FRIEND
_____

_____

_____

_____

DO LATER

_____

_____

_____

_____

_____

DO NOW
(80% of productivity)

_____

_____

_____

_____

_____

_____

_____

_____

_____

_____

_____

_____

EVENING REFLECTION: Good Things That Happened Today

_____

_____

DATE:

MORNING AFFIRMATION:

_____

_____

I'M GRATEFUL FOR:

_____

_____

_____

DAILY GOALS

MANDATORY

_____
JOURNAL
_____
WORKOUT
_____
QUALITY TIME FAMILY/FRIEND
_____
_____
_____
_____

DO LATER

_____
_____
_____
_____
_____
_____

DO NOW
(80% of productivity)

_____
_____
_____
_____
_____
_____
_____
_____
_____
_____
_____
_____

EVENING REFLECTION: Good Things That Happened Today

_____

_____

DATE:

MORNING AFFIRMATION:

_____

_____

I'M GRATEFUL FOR:

_____

_____

_____

DAILY GOALS

MANDATORY

_____
JOURNAL
_____
WORKOUT
_____
QUALITY TIME FAMILY/FRIEND
_____

_____

_____

DO LATER

_____

_____

_____

_____

_____

_____

DO NOW
(80% of productivity)

_____

_____

_____

_____

_____

_____

_____

_____

_____

_____

_____

_____

_____

EVENING REFLECTION: Good Things That Happened Today

_____

_____

DATE:

MORNING AFFIRMATION:

_____

_____

I'M GRATEFUL FOR:

_____

_____

_____

DAILY GOALS

MANDATORY

_____
JOURNAL
_____
WORKOUT
_____
QUALITY TIME FAMILY/FRIEND
_____
_____
_____
_____
_____

DO LATER

_____
_____
_____
_____
_____
_____

DO NOW
(80% of productivity)

_____
_____
_____
_____
_____
_____
_____
_____
_____
_____
_____
_____
_____
_____

EVENING REFLECTION: Good Things That Happened Today

_____

_____

DATE:

MORNING AFFIRMATION:

_____

_____

I'M GRATEFUL FOR:

_____

_____

_____

DAILY GOALS

MANDATORY

DO NOW
(80% of productivity)

_____
JOURNAL
_____
WORKOUT
_____
QUALITY TIME FAMILY/FRIEND
_____
_____
_____
_____

DO LATER

_____
_____
_____
_____
_____
_____
_____

_____
_____
_____
_____
_____
_____
_____
_____
_____
_____
_____
_____

EVENING REFLECTION: Good Things That Happened Today

_____

_____

DATE:

MORNING AFFIRMATION:

_____

_____

I'M GRATEFUL FOR:

_____

_____

_____

DAILY GOALS

MANDATORY	DO NOW
	(80% of productivity)

MANDATORY

_____
JOURNAL
_____
WORKOUT
_____
QUALITY TIME FAMILY/FRIEND
_____

_____

_____

_____

DO LATER

_____

_____

_____

_____

_____

_____

DO NOW
(80% of productivity)

_____

_____

_____

_____

_____

_____

_____

_____

_____

_____

_____

EVENING REFLECTION: Good Things That Happened Today

_____

_____

DATE:

MORNING AFFIRMATION:

_____

_____

I'M GRATEFUL FOR:

_____

_____

_____

DAILY GOALS

MANDATORY

DO NOW
(80% of productivity)

JOURNAL

WORKOUT

QUALITY TIME FAMILY/FRIEND

DO LATER

EVENING REFLECTION: Good Things That Happened Today

_____

_____

DATE:

MORNING AFFIRMATION:

_____

_____

I'M GRATEFUL FOR:

_____

_____

_____

DAILY GOALS

MANDATORY

_____
JOURNAL
_____
WORKOUT
_____
QUALITY TIME FAMILY/FRIEND
_____
_____
_____
_____

DO LATER

_____
_____
_____
_____
_____
_____

DO NOW
(80% of productivity)

_____
_____
_____
_____
_____
_____
_____
_____
_____
_____
_____
_____
_____
_____

EVENING REFLECTION: Good Things That Happened Today

_____

_____

DATE:

MORNING AFFIRMATION:

_____

_____

I'M GRATEFUL FOR:

_____

_____

_____

DAILY GOALS

MANDATORY

_____
JOURNAL
_____
WORKOUT
_____
QUALITY TIME FAMILY/FRIEND
_____
_____
_____
_____

DO LATER

_____
_____
_____
_____
_____

DO NOW
(80% of productivity)

_____
_____
_____
_____
_____
_____
_____
_____
_____
_____
_____
_____
_____
_____

EVENING REFLECTION: Good Things That Happened Today

_____

_____

DATE:

MORNING AFFIRMATION:

_____

_____

I'M GRATEFUL FOR:

_____

_____

_____

DAILY GOALS

MANDATORY	DO NOW
	(80% of productivity)

MANDATORY

_____

JOURNAL
_____
WORKOUT
_____
QUALITY TIME FAMILY/FRIEND
_____

_____

_____

DO LATER

_____

_____

_____

_____

_____

DO NOW
(80% of productivity)

_____

_____

_____

_____

_____

_____

_____

_____

_____

_____

_____

EVENING REFLECTION: Good Things That Happened Today

_____

_____

DATE:

MORNING AFFIRMATION:

_____

_____

I'M GRATEFUL FOR:

_____

_____

_____

DAILY GOALS

MANDATORY

_____
JOURNAL
_____
WORKOUT
_____
QUALITY TIME FAMILY/FRIEND
_____
_____
_____
_____
_____

DO LATER

_____
_____
_____
_____
_____
_____
_____
_____

DO NOW
(80% of productivity)

_____
_____
_____
_____
_____
_____
_____
_____
_____
_____
_____
_____

EVENING REFLECTION: Good Things That Happened Today

_____

_____

DATE:

MORNING AFFIRMATION:

_____

_____

I'M GRATEFUL FOR:

_____

_____

_____

DAILY GOALS

MANDATORY

_____
JOURNAL
_____
WORKOUT
_____
QUALITY TIME FAMILY/FRIEND
_____
_____
_____
_____

DO LATER

_____
_____
_____
_____
_____
_____

DO NOW
(80% of productivity)

_____
_____
_____
_____
_____
_____
_____
_____
_____
_____
_____

EVENING REFLECTION: Good Things That Happened Today

_____

_____

DATE:

MORNING AFFIRMATION:

_____

_____

I'M GRATEFUL FOR:

_____

_____

_____

DAILY GOALS

MANDATORY

DO NOW
(80% of productivity)

_____
JOURNAL
_____
WORKOUT
_____
QUALITY TIME FAMILY/FRIEND
_____
_____
_____
_____

_____
_____
_____
_____
_____

DO LATER

_____
_____
_____
_____
_____
_____

_____
_____
_____
_____
_____
_____

EVENING REFLECTION: Good Things That Happened Today

_____

_____

DATE:

MORNING AFFIRMATION:

_____
_____

I'M GRATEFUL FOR:

_____
_____
_____

DAILY GOALS

MANDATORY

_____
JOURNAL
_____
WORKOUT
_____
QUALITY TIME FAMILY/FRIEND
_____
_____
_____
_____

DO LATER

_____
_____
_____
_____
_____
_____

DO NOW
(80% of productivity)

_____
_____
_____
_____
_____
_____
_____
_____
_____
_____
_____

EVENING REFLECTION: Good Things That Happened Today

_____
_____

DATE:

MORNING AFFIRMATION:

_____

_____

I'M GRATEFUL FOR:

_____

_____

_____

DAILY GOALS

MANDATORY

_____
JOURNAL
_____
WORKOUT
_____
QUALITY TIME FAMILY/FRIEND
_____
_____
_____
_____
_____

DO LATER

_____
_____
_____
_____
_____
_____
_____

DO NOW
(80% of productivity)

_____
_____
_____
_____
_____
_____
_____
_____
_____
_____
_____
_____
_____
_____
_____
_____
_____

EVENING REFLECTION: Good Things That Happened Today

_____

_____

DATE:

MORNING AFFIRMATION:

_____

_____

I'M GRATEFUL FOR:

_____

_____

_____

DAILY GOALS

MANDATORY	DO NOW
	(80% of productivity)

MANDATORY

JOURNAL

WORKOUT

QUALITY TIME FAMILY/FRIEND

_____

_____

_____

DO LATER

_____

_____

_____

_____

_____

EVENING REFLECTION: Good Things That Happened Today

_____

_____

DATE:

MORNING AFFIRMATION:

_____

_____

I'M GRATEFUL FOR:

_____

_____

_____

DAILY GOALS

MANDATORY

DO NOW
(80% of productivity)

_____
JOURNAL
_____
WORKOUT
_____
QUALITY TIME FAMILY/FRIEND
_____
_____
_____
_____
_____

DO LATER

_____
_____
_____
_____
_____
_____
_____

_____
_____
_____
_____
_____
_____
_____
_____
_____
_____
_____

EVENING REFLECTION: Good Things That Happened Today

_____

_____

DATE:

MORNING AFFIRMATION:

_____

_____

I'M GRATEFUL FOR:

_____

_____

_____

DAILY GOALS

MANDATORY

DO NOW
(80% of productivity)

_____
JOURNAL
_____
WORKOUT
_____
QUALITY TIME FAMILY/FRIEND
_____
_____
_____
_____

_____
_____
_____
_____
_____
_____

DO LATER

_____
_____
_____
_____
_____
_____
_____

_____
_____
_____
_____
_____
_____

EVENING REFLECTION: Good Things That Happened Today

_____

_____

DATE:

MORNING AFFIRMATION:

_____
_____

I'M GRATEFUL FOR:

_____
_____
_____

DAILY GOALS

MANDATORY

_____
JOURNAL
WORKOUT
QUALITY TIME FAMILY/FRIEND
_____
_____
_____
_____

DO LATER

_____
_____
_____
_____
_____
_____
_____

DO NOW
(80% of productivity)

_____
_____
_____
_____
_____
_____
_____
_____
_____
_____
_____
_____
_____

EVENING REFLECTION: Good Things That Happened Today

_____
_____

DATE:

MORNING AFFIRMATION:

_____

_____

I'M GRATEFUL FOR:

_____

_____

_____

DAILY GOALS

MANDATORY

JOURNAL

WORKOUT

QUALITY TIME FAMILY/FRIEND

_____

_____

_____

DO LATER

_____

_____

_____

_____

_____

_____

DO NOW
(80% of productivity)

_____

_____

_____

_____

_____

_____

_____

_____

_____

_____

_____

_____

_____

EVENING REFLECTION: Good Things That Happened Today

_____

_____

MORNING AFFIRMATION:

_____

_____

I'M GRATEFUL FOR:

_____

_____

_____

DAILY GOALS

MANDATORY

DO NOW
(80% of productivity)

JOURNAL

WORKOUT

QUALITY TIME FAMILY/FRIEND

_____

_____

_____

_____

DO LATER

_____

_____

_____

_____

_____

_____

EVENING REFLECTION: Good Things That Happened Today

_____

_____

DATE:

MORNING AFFIRMATION:

_____

_____

I'M GRATEFUL FOR:

_____

_____

_____

DAILY GOALS

MANDATORY

_____
JOURNAL
_____
WORKOUT
_____
QUALITY TIME FAMILY/FRIEND
_____
_____
_____
_____

DO LATER

_____
_____
_____
_____
_____
_____
_____

DO NOW
(80% of productivity)

_____
_____
_____
_____
_____
_____
_____
_____
_____
_____
_____
_____
_____
_____

EVENING REFLECTION: Good Things That Happened Today

_____

_____

DATE:

MORNING AFFIRMATION:

_____

_____

I'M GRATEFUL FOR:

_____

_____

_____

DAILY GOALS

MANDATORY

DO NOW
(80% of productivity)

_____
JOURNAL
_____
WORKOUT
_____
QUALITY TIME FAMILY/FRIEND
_____

_____

_____

_____

_____

DO LATER

_____

_____

_____

_____

_____

_____

_____

_____

_____

_____

_____

_____

_____

_____

_____

_____

_____

_____

EVENING REFLECTION: Good Things That Happened Today

_____

_____

DATE:

MORNING AFFIRMATION:

_____

_____

I'M GRATEFUL FOR:

_____

_____

_____

DAILY GOALS

MANDATORY

DO NOW
(80% of productivity)

_____
JOURNAL
_____
WORKOUT
_____
QUALITY TIME FAMILY/FRIEND
_____
_____
_____
_____
_____

DO LATER

_____
_____
_____
_____
_____
_____
_____
_____

_____
_____
_____
_____
_____
_____
_____
_____
_____
_____
_____
_____

EVENING REFLECTION: Good Things That Happened Today

_____

_____

DATE:

MORNING AFFIRMATION:

_____

_____

I'M GRATEFUL FOR:

_____

_____

_____

DAILY GOALS

MANDATORY	DO NOW
	(80% of productivity)

MANDATORY

_____

JOURNAL

_____

WORKOUT

_____

QUALITY TIME FAMILY/FRIEND

_____

_____

_____

_____

DO LATER

_____

_____

_____

_____

_____

_____

DO NOW
(80% of productivity)

_____

_____

_____

_____

_____

_____

_____

_____

_____

_____

_____

_____

_____

EVENING REFLECTION: Good Things That Happened Today

_____

_____

DATE:

MORNING AFFIRMATION:

_____

_____

I'M GRATEFUL FOR:

_____

_____

_____

DAILY GOALS

MANDATORY

DO NOW
(80% of productivity)

_____
JOURNAL
_____
WORKOUT
_____
QUALITY TIME FAMILY/FRIEND
_____
_____
_____
_____

DO LATER

_____
_____
_____
_____
_____
_____
_____

EVENING REFLECTION: Good Things That Happened Today

_____

_____

DATE:

MORNING AFFIRMATION:

_____

_____

I'M GRATEFUL FOR:

_____

_____

_____

DAILY GOALS

MANDATORY

_____

JOURNAL

WORKOUT

QUALITY TIME FAMILY/FRIEND

_____

_____

_____

_____

DO LATER

_____

_____

_____

_____

_____

DO NOW
(80% of productivity)

_____

_____

_____

_____

_____

_____

_____

_____

_____

_____

_____

_____

_____

EVENING REFLECTION: Good Things That Happened Today

_____

_____

DATE:

MORNING AFFIRMATION:

_____

_____

I'M GRATEFUL FOR:

_____

_____

_____

DAILY GOALS

MANDATORY

_____
JOURNAL
_____
WORKOUT
_____
QUALITY TIME FAMILY/FRIEND
_____
_____
_____
_____

DO LATER

_____
_____
_____
_____
_____
_____

DO NOW
(80% of productivity)

_____
_____
_____
_____
_____
_____
_____
_____
_____
_____
_____
_____

EVENING REFLECTION: Good Things That Happened Today

_____

_____

MORNING AFFIRMATION:

_____

_____

I'M GRATEFUL FOR:

_____

_____

_____

DAILY GOALS

MANDATORY

_____
JOURNAL
_____
WORKOUT
_____
QUALITY TIME FAMILY/FRIEND
_____
_____
_____
_____

DO LATER

_____
_____
_____
_____
_____
_____
_____

DO NOW
(80% of productivity)

_____
_____
_____
_____
_____
_____
_____
_____
_____
_____
_____
_____
_____
_____

EVENING REFLECTION: Good Things That Happened Today

_____

_____

DATE:

MORNING AFFIRMATION:

_____

_____

I'M GRATEFUL FOR:

_____

_____

_____

DAILY GOALS

MANDATORY

DO NOW
(80% of productivity)

_____

JOURNAL

WORKOUT

QUALITY TIME FAMILY/FRIEND

_____

_____

_____

_____

DO LATER

_____

_____

_____

_____

_____

_____

_____

DO NOW (80% of productivity)

_____

_____

_____

_____

_____

_____

_____

_____

_____

_____

_____

_____

EVENING REFLECTION: Good Things That Happened Today

_____

_____

DATE:

MORNING AFFIRMATION:

_____

_____

I'M GRATEFUL FOR:

_____

_____

_____

DAILY GOALS

MANDATORY	DO NOW
	(80% of productivity)

MANDATORY

JOURNAL

WORKOUT

QUALITY TIME FAMILY/FRIEND

_____

_____

_____

DO NOW
(80% of productivity)

DO LATER

EVENING REFLECTION: Good Things That Happened Today

_____

_____

MORNING AFFIRMATION:

_____

_____

I'M GRATEFUL FOR:

_____

_____

_____

DAILY GOALS

MANDATORY	DO NOW
	(80% of productivity)

MANDATORY

_____
JOURNAL
_____
WORKOUT
_____
QUALITY TIME FAMILY/FRIEND
_____
_____
_____
_____

DO LATER

_____
_____
_____
_____
_____
_____
_____

DO NOW
(80% of productivity)

_____
_____
_____
_____
_____
_____
_____
_____
_____
_____
_____
_____
_____

EVENING REFLECTION: Good Things That Happened Today

_____

_____

DATE:

MORNING AFFIRMATION:

_____

_____

I'M GRATEFUL FOR:

_____

_____

_____

DAILY GOALS

MANDATORY	DO NOW
	(80% of productivity)

MANDATORY

JOURNAL

WORKOUT

QUALITY TIME FAMILY/FRIEND

_____

_____

_____

DO LATER

_____

_____

_____

_____

_____

_____

DO NOW
(80% of productivity)

_____

_____

_____

_____

_____

_____

_____

_____

_____

_____

_____

_____

EVENING REFLECTION: Good Things That Happened Today

_____

_____

DATE:

MORNING AFFIRMATION:

_____

_____

I'M GRATEFUL FOR:

_____

_____

_____

DAILY GOALS

MANDATORY

JOURNAL

WORKOUT

QUALITY TIME FAMILY/FRIEND

_____

_____

_____

DO LATER

_____

_____

_____

_____

_____

_____

_____

DO NOW
(80% of productivity)

_____

_____

_____

_____

_____

_____

_____

_____

_____

_____

_____

_____

EVENING REFLECTION: Good Things That Happened Today

_____

_____

DATE:

MORNING AFFIRMATION:

_____

_____

I'M GRATEFUL FOR:

_____

_____

DAILY GOALS

MANDATORY

_____
JOURNAL
_____
WORKOUT
_____
QUALITY TIME FAMILY/FRIEND
_____
_____
_____
_____
_____

DO LATER

_____
_____
_____
_____
_____
_____
_____

DO NOW
(80% of productivity)

_____
_____
_____
_____
_____
_____
_____
_____
_____
_____
_____
_____
_____
_____
_____

EVENING REFLECTION: Good Things That Happened Today

_____

_____

DATE:

MORNING AFFIRMATION:

_____

_____

I'M GRATEFUL FOR:

_____

_____

DAILY GOALS

MANDATORY

_____

JOURNAL

WORKOUT

QUALITY TIME FAMILY/FRIEND

_____

_____

_____

_____

DO LATER

_____

_____

_____

_____

_____

_____

_____

DO NOW
(80% of productivity)

_____

_____

_____

_____

_____

_____

_____

_____

_____

_____

_____

_____

_____

_____

EVENING REFLECTION: Good Things That Happened Today

_____

_____

MORNING AFFIRMATION:

_____

_____

I'M GRATEFUL FOR:

_____

_____

_____

DAILY GOALS

MANDATORY

_____

JOURNAL

_____

WORKOUT

_____

QUALITY TIME FAMILY/FRIEND

_____

_____

_____

_____

DO LATER

_____

_____

_____

_____

_____

_____

DO NOW
(80% of productivity)

_____

_____

_____

_____

_____

_____

_____

_____

_____

_____

_____

_____

_____

EVENING REFLECTION: Good Things That Happened Today

_____

_____

DATE:

MORNING AFFIRMATION:

_____

_____

I'M GRATEFUL FOR:

_____

_____

_____

DAILY GOALS

MANDATORY

DO NOW
(80% of productivity)

JOURNAL

WORKOUT

QUALITY TIME FAMILY/FRIEND

_____

_____

_____

_____

DO LATER

_____

_____

_____

_____

_____

_____

_____

EVENING REFLECTION: Good Things That Happened Today

_____

_____

DATE:

MORNING AFFIRMATION:

_____

_____

I'M GRATEFUL FOR:

_____

_____

_____

DAILY GOALS

MANDATORY

_____
JOURNAL
_____
WORKOUT
_____
QUALITY TIME FAMILY/FRIEND
_____

_____

_____

_____

DO LATER

_____

_____

_____

_____

_____

_____

DO NOW
(80% of productivity)

_____

_____

_____

_____

_____

_____

_____

_____

_____

_____

_____

_____

EVENING REFLECTION: Good Things That Happened Today

_____

_____

DATE:

MORNING AFFIRMATION:

_____

_____

I'M GRATEFUL FOR:

_____

_____

_____

DAILY GOALS

MANDATORY

_____
JOURNAL
WORKOUT
QUALITY TIME FAMILY/FRIEND
_____
_____
_____
_____

DO LATER

_____

_____

_____

_____

_____

_____

DO NOW
(80% of productivity)

_____

_____

_____

_____

_____

_____

_____

_____

_____

_____

EVENING REFLECTION: Good Things That Happened Today

_____

_____

DATE:

MORNING AFFIRMATION:

_____

_____

I'M GRATEFUL FOR:

_____

_____

_____

DAILY GOALS

MANDATORY

DO NOW
(80% of productivity)

_____
JOURNAL
_____
WORKOUT
_____
QUALITY TIME FAMILY/FRIEND
_____
_____
_____
_____
_____

DO LATER

_____
_____
_____
_____
_____
_____
_____

_____
_____
_____
_____
_____
_____
_____
_____
_____
_____
_____

EVENING REFLECTION: Good Things That Happened Today

_____

_____

DATE:

MORNING AFFIRMATION:

_____

_____

I'M GRATEFUL FOR:

_____

_____

_____

DAILY GOALS

MANDATORY

_____
JOURNAL
_____
WORKOUT
_____
QUALITY TIME FAMILY/FRIEND
_____
_____
_____
_____

DO LATER

_____
_____
_____
_____
_____
_____

DO NOW
(80% of productivity)

_____
_____
_____
_____
_____
_____
_____
_____
_____
_____
_____
_____

EVENING REFLECTION: Good Things That Happened Today

_____

_____

DATE:

MORNING AFFIRMATION:

_____

_____

I'M GRATEFUL FOR:

_____

_____

_____

DAILY GOALS

MANDATORY

DO NOW
(80% of productivity)

JOURNAL

WORKOUT

QUALITY TIME FAMILY/FRIEND

_____

_____

_____

DO LATER

_____

_____

_____

_____

_____

EVENING REFLECTION: Good Things That Happened Today

_____

_____

DATE:

MORNING AFFIRMATION:

_____

_____

I'M GRATEFUL FOR:

_____

_____

_____

DAILY GOALS

MANDATORY

DO NOW
(80% of productivity)

_____
JOURNAL
_____
WORKOUT
_____
QUALITY TIME FAMILY/FRIEND
_____

_____
_____
_____
_____

DO LATER

_____
_____
_____
_____
_____
_____

_____
_____
_____
_____
_____
_____
_____
_____
_____
_____

EVENING REFLECTION: Good Things That Happened Today

_____

_____

DATE:

MORNING AFFIRMATION:

_____

_____

I'M GRATEFUL FOR:

_____

_____

_____

DAILY GOALS

MANDATORY

DO NOW
(80% of productivity)

_____
JOURNAL
_____
WORKOUT
_____
QUALITY TIME FAMILY/FRIEND
_____
_____
_____
_____

DO LATER

_____
_____
_____
_____
_____
_____
_____

_____
_____
_____
_____
_____
_____
_____
_____
_____
_____
_____
_____
_____

EVENING REFLECTION: Good Things That Happened Today

_____

_____

DATE:

MORNING AFFIRMATION:

_____

_____

I'M GRATEFUL FOR:

_____

_____

_____

DAILY GOALS

MANDATORY		DO NOW
		(80% of productivity)
JOURNAL		
WORKOUT		
QUALITY TIME FAMILY/FRIEND		

DO LATER

EVENING REFLECTION: Good Things That Happened Today

_____

_____

DATE:

MORNING AFFIRMATION:

_____

_____

I'M GRATEFUL FOR:

_____

_____

_____

DAILY GOALS

MANDATORY

_____
JOURNAL
_____
WORKOUT
_____
QUALITY TIME FAMILY/FRIEND
_____
_____
_____
_____
_____

DO LATER

_____
_____
_____
_____
_____
_____
_____

DO NOW
(80% of productivity)

_____
_____
_____
_____
_____
_____
_____
_____
_____
_____
_____
_____
_____
_____
_____

EVENING REFLECTION: Good Things That Happened Today

_____

_____

DATE:

MORNING AFFIRMATION:

_____

_____

I'M GRATEFUL FOR:

_____

_____

_____

DAILY GOALS

MANDATORY	DO NOW
	(80% of productivity)

MANDATORY

_____

JOURNAL

_____

WORKOUT

_____

QUALITY TIME FAMILY/FRIEND

_____

_____

_____

_____

DO LATER

_____

_____

_____

_____

_____

_____

DO NOW
(80% of productivity)

_____

_____

_____

_____

_____

_____

_____

_____

_____

_____

_____

EVENING REFLECTION: Good Things That Happened Today

_____

_____

DATE:

MORNING AFFIRMATION:

_____

_____

I'M GRATEFUL FOR:

_____

_____

_____

DAILY GOALS

MANDATORY

DO NOW
(80% of productivity)

_____

JOURNAL

WORKOUT

QUALITY TIME FAMILY/FRIEND

_____

_____

_____

DO LATER

_____

_____

_____

_____

_____

_____

EVENING REFLECTION: Good Things That Happened Today

_____

_____

DATE:

MORNING AFFIRMATION:

_____

_____

I'M GRATEFUL FOR:

_____

_____

_____

DAILY GOALS

MANDATORY	DO NOW
	(80% of productivity)

MANDATORY
_____
JOURNAL
WORKOUT
QUALITY TIME FAMILY/FRIEND
_____
_____
_____
_____

DO LATER
_____
_____
_____
_____
_____
_____

DO NOW
(80% of productivity)
_____
_____
_____
_____
_____
_____
_____
_____
_____
_____
_____
_____
_____

EVENING REFLECTION: Good Things That Happened Today

_____

_____

DATE:

MORNING AFFIRMATION:

_____

_____

I'M GRATEFUL FOR:

_____

_____

_____

DAILY GOALS

MANDATORY

_____

JOURNAL

_____

WORKOUT

_____

QUALITY TIME FAMILY/FRIEND

_____

_____

_____

_____

DO LATER

_____

_____

_____

_____

_____

_____

DO NOW
(80% of productivity)

_____

_____

_____

_____

_____

_____

_____

_____

_____

_____

_____

_____

EVENING REFLECTION: Good Things That Happened Today

_____

_____

DATE:

MORNING AFFIRMATION:

_____

_____

I'M GRATEFUL FOR:

_____

_____

_____

DAILY GOALS

MANDATORY

_____
JOURNAL
_____
WORKOUT
_____
QUALITY TIME FAMILY/FRIEND
_____
_____
_____
_____

DO LATER

_____
_____
_____
_____
_____
_____

DO NOW
(80% of productivity)

_____
_____
_____
_____
_____
_____
_____
_____
_____
_____
_____

EVENING REFLECTION: Good Things That Happened Today

_____

_____

Affirmation Ideas When You Need a Boost

1. I am grounded and fully present in this moment.
2. I trust in my ability to handle life's ups and downs.
3. I am resilient and can handle whatever comes my way.
4. I release all negative energy that is holding me back.
5. I am in control of my thoughts and emotions.
6. I am worthy of love, success, and happiness.
7. I am growing and becoming a better version of myself every day.
8. I am focused, clear-minded, and ready to take on the day.
9. I respect my emotional needs.
10. I am deserving of good things and positive energy.
11. I am full of courage and move forward fearlessly.
12. I am exactly where I need to be, trusting the process.
13. I am capable of creating the life I desire.
14. I am releasing what I cannot control and embracing what I can.
15. I value my own opinions and ideas.
16. I am powerful, confident, and unstoppable.
17. I am letting go of what no longer serves me.
18. I choose to focus on the good in my life.
19. I am open to all the opportunities today brings.
20. I am worthy of taking up space and using my voice.
21. I am embracing each challenge as an opportunity for growth.
22. I am surrounded by love, strength, and positivity.
23. I am proud of all that I've accomplished and will continue to achieve.
24. I am allowing myself to acknowledge all unpleasant emotions, not judge them as good or bad, but as a human experience.
25. I am allowing myself to feel and then release.
26. I am attracting productivity, creativity, and clarity.
27. I am grateful for who I am and all that I have.
28. I am embracing self-love and kindness in all I do.
29. Life always gives me what I need.
30. I am creating my own peace, no matter what's around me.

Made in the USA
Las Vegas, NV
05 May 2025

21792137R00039